Successful Bodybuilding
With
Machines

By Master HIT Trainer
David Groscup
IART CFC, IART/Med-Ex High Intensity Trainer
http://drhitshighintensitybodybuilding.blogspot.com/

Dr HIT'S Ultimate BodyBuilding Guide

High Intensity Methods For Rapid Muscle Growth: Arms

David Groscup

Dr HIT'S Ultimate BodyBuilding Guide

High Intensity Methods For Rapid Muscle Growth: Chest

David Groscup

Dr HIT's Effective High Intensity Variables

Add Muscle Fast With Today's Best Bodybuilding Method!

David Groscup

The Training Bible: Proven Programs to Lose Weight, Tone, Strengthen And Build Muscle

David Groscup
IART CFC
IART/MED-EX HIT Training Specialist

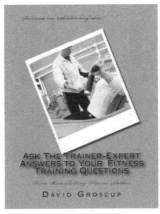

Ask The Trainer-Expert Answers to Your Fitness Training Questions

From Best-Selling Fitness Author

David Groscup

Table of Contents

Traditionally, bodybuilding has been, and still is, done by using barbells and dumbbells to build and shape muscle. This changed somewhat with the advent of Nautilus machines in the mid seventies and Nautilus fitness centers soon after. Many fitness enthusiasts and bodybuilders tried the machines and were surprised at the many positive results they obtained from training with these new devices.

Owner/inventor Arthur Jones, promoted his machines as being an improvement over the barbell and dumbbells everyone had been using to that point. His reasoning was that by developing specialized cams for his machines that maximized strength profiles for specific muscles and allowing movement through proper motion, he could develop strength and muscle better and faster than anyone was able to do prior with barbells and dumbbells.

As you can image, he met with strong resistance from the bodybuilding community who rejected his intrusion into their established training regimens. To make matters worse, he promoted his machines with a training program that was based upon brief, intense workouts, which also was a radical departure from the norm at that time.

To prove the effectiveness of his equipment and his training program, he enlisted a young bodybuilder, Casey Viator to train under his guidance. Viator went on to win the Mr. America at the young age of 19, a feat never duplicated to this day. He experienced rapid muscle gains in the neighborhood of 63 pounds and lost 18 pounds of fat in four weeks,with a total of 14 workout sessions.

These results are incredible for anyone, even Viator, whose genetics were perfect for bodybuilding. Some of the gains in muscle were a result of "muscle memory", in which the body regains lost muscle tissue that it had in the past. Viator had injured himself in an industrial accident and hadn't been able to train for some time.

Mr. Jones used this success as a promotional tool for his Nautilus Machines and worked with Ellington Darden to perfect training routines and principles for them. Full body routines were the result, where each muscle group beginning with the largest and working down to the smallest were trained with two sets total.

One set of two exercises was utilized in a pre-exhaust fashion. (See my Dr. HIT's Effective Training Variables book.) This was effective to a point but offered limited concentration on training individual muscles for maximum muscle growth. To train a muscle with maximum intensity it is necessary to train it while fresh first or second in a workout, which is impossible with a full body routine.

Bodybuilders had migrated to split routines by this time where the body was divided into different training days. Some trained with a push-pull system, training all muscles involved in pushing movements on one day and muscles used to push on another. Other methods to divide training include arms and shoulders, chest and back, legs and abs.

Goal of this book

The purpose of this book is to give you, the reader, new ideas and techniques to make use of the great advantages weight machines offer. Whether you are a bodybuilder, athlete in another sport, fitness enthusiast or mom trying to get back in shape, machines offer the safest, most effective way to get results fast.

After explaining features of certain machines, complete workouts will be outlined and explained in full. The focus will be on HIT, or high intensity training principals because in my experience that is the most efficient way to get in shape and build strength and muscle size.

Evolution of machine development

As mentioned previously, Nautilus was the equipment company most responsible for popularizing the use of weight machines. With the success of Nautilus, other equipment manufacturers appeared on the scene. These included Cybex, Stride, Life Fitness, Precor, Pro Maxima and many more. Most of these machines were very well made and of industrial grade durability.

The original Nautilus machines got their name from the cams that were an integral part of their design and function. They were made from polished aluminum and had small circles etched in them. The important features of the cam were its shape and size, which were designed to maximize a muscle's strength curve to eliminate sticking points and train a muscle through the full movement of an exercise. First generation models used thick chains to move the weight stack. Cables replaced the chains briefly before Kevlar belts replaced them. Kevlar belts aren't prone to stretching and offer quiet, smooth operation.

The newest Nautilus machines have eliminated the large cams and replaced them with smaller cams, which are as effective as the original ones because of the altered design of the pulley systems. There is a machine or two for each muscle group so the entire body can be trained effectively.

The original models were large hulks that took up a lot of space on a gym floor and had two machines on each station, one for an isolation exercise and another for a compound one. New models have drastically reduced the need for floor space and are stand-alone machines, which offer one exercise per machine. Several different lines of machines are available.

Cybex is another company that manufactures a full line of high quality machines and is known for producing heavily built, durable models. They use Kevlar belts to drive the weight stack like Nautilus.

Strive, which is headquartered in McMurray, PA, offers a line of machines with adjustable cams, allowing the user to focus on different zones of an exercise to maximize muscle development.

There are well over 100 different manufacturers proving the popularity of selectorized stack machines.

Advantages of machines

Some of the advantages of training with machines are:

- Lack of need to balance the weight.
- Proper form in an exercise. The machine will only allow an exercise to be done through a defined motion. This is especially beneficial for new trainees who are more likely to get injured due to poor exercise form.
- Easy to use high intensity variables such as forced reps, negatives and the like.
- Safe use of weights. If a weight becomes too heavy you return it to the stack. Free weights often necessitate a spotter for safe use to prevent dropping the weight on yourself.

Types of machines

The different types of weight machines are cable machines, free weight loaded, selectorized and smith. They are all effective at building muscle and offer great variety to your training.

Cable machines have been around for a long time and allow the user to mimic almost every free weight movement with the ease of use of a selectorized machine. Many accessories are available for cable machines and include various handles, bars and ropes. Models are available that offer adjustable placement of pulleys so the user can use low, mid and high pulley level exercises. They offer selectorized weight stacks for easy weight selection.

Single station machines focus on one muscle group and offer one exercise per machine. They are all commercial heavy grade and are very effective at building strength and muscle size. They offer selectorized weight stacks for easy weight selection.

Plate loaded machines are similar to selectorized stack machines with the exception that it is necessary to load the machine with barbell plates for resistance. Some bodybuilders feel they offer better balance than their selectorized counterparts because of weight stack friction but I feel that is a mute point that I've never found noticeable on good selectorized machines.

Smith machines are similar to power racks except the bar is mounted on a vertical set of bars and offers pins located a couple of inches apart that allow the user to rack the weight easily. There are safety catches that stop the weight from descending if it is dropped, making it much safer than free weight barbell use and eliminating the need for spotters even on heavy exercises like squats and bench presses.

Hydraulic machines use either water or hydraulic fluid pressure to add resistance to the movement arms. These machines aren't very popular therefore you won't see them in most gyms. I don't recommend them because it is hard to correlate resistance levels to weight and I am not enthusiastic about about the lack of negative resistance because the negative portion of an exercise is very important to strength and muscle growth.

All of the machines offer advantages that can be used to make your fitness and bodybuilding training more productive. If you have nagging injuries, selectorized, single station machines are best due to their safe operation.

Definition of terms

Forced reps-This is the most popular high intensity variable. It is done as follows: After taking a set of an exercise to muscular failure your training partner provides just enough assistance to allow you to complete additional reps. This is done by him/her pressing two or three fingers on the bar or machine handle and applying adequate pressure to facilitate completion of the desired reps.

Pure negative reps- These are great for safely placing a heavy resistance load on a muscle. Typically you can use 40% more weight than you can during normal rep sets. The purest way to do these reps is to have a partner raise the weight to the finish point of an exercise then lower it under your own power slowly, often to account of 8.

Negative-accentuated reps- These are similar to pure negative reps except it is unnecessary to have a partner to do them. Using the leg press as an example, press the footplate to the end and resist the weight with your left leg only. Repeat, resisting the weight with your right leg only. This constitutes one cycle.

Omni-contraction reps- After completing the positive portion of a rep, lower the weight one third of the way and do a 10 second static hold. Lower the weight to mid-point and do another 10 second hold. Finish the rep by doing a 10 second hold at the end of the negative.

Rest-pause reps- Load the weight with a maximum weight that allows you to barely complete one rep. Rest for 10 seconds then do a second single, maximal rep. Continue until finishing a set of the desired amount of single reps.

Partial reps- These are done by dividing a complete rep into different zones. As an example, divide the machine curl into three equal portions. Complete the desired amount of reps in each zone before training the next zone or completing full, complete reps. These are great for focusing your efforts on different areas of an exercise to work past a sticking point. This variable allows you to reap a lot of the benefits only available with properly cammed machines and there is an infinite amount of variations that can be done.

Static Holds- One of the newer HIT variables, these are done in several different ways. The most popular is to select a weight that allows you to hold it in the position of full contraction for 20 seconds before beginning to fail. Rest 10 seconds before reducing the weight and completing a second hold. Complete a series of single holds to constitute one set. This can also be done pyramid style by beginning with a lower sub-maximum weight and working your way up the stack until hitting your max weight then working your way back down the stack.

Machine routines using the HIT protocol

Legs

- leg extensions- 1 set of 15 reps

Select a moderate weight and extend the arms of the machine to full extension with your legs and tense your thigh muscles hard to activate additional muscle fibers before returning to the start position to begin the next rep.

- leg press- 1 set of 10 negative reps

Select a weight that is 40% heavier than you typically use in this exercise. Have a training partner assist you in pressing the weight to the fully extended position. Lower the weight under your own power to a count of 8. Continue until you have completed a total of 10 negative reps.

- leg extensions- 1 set of 10 static holds

Select a weight that allows maximum effort in holding the arms of the machine in the fully-contracted position for 10 seconds. Extend the machine arms to the end point of the exercise and hold for 10 seconds before returning to the beginning. Rest 10 seconds then complete a second hold.

This brief routine is highly effective because of the high intensity used to train the muscles. It trained all three of the muscle strengths: concentric or positive, eccentric or negative and static or holding. This maximizes fiber use and breaks the muscles down thoroughly.

Chest

- machine flyes or pek dek- 1 set of 15 reps

These are to be done omni-contraction style. On each rep lower the arms slowly, stop a third of the way and hold the arms for 10 seconds. Lower to the middle position and hold the weight for 10 seconds. To complete the rep, lower the weight to the beginning position and hold the weight for 10 seconds. Repeat this for each additional rep in the set.

- machine dips- 1 set of 8 rest pause reps + static holds

Select a weight that is near your 1RM and push the arms down to the pre-lockout position and hold for 10 seconds before returning the weight to the stack. Rest for 10 seconds before completing the second rep in the same fashion. Do an additional 6 reps to finish the set. It is important to lean forward when doing dips to focus on the chest and lessen the workload on the triceps muscles.

- machine bench press- 1 set of 8 reps + 4 negative reps

Use either a flat bench press machine or one that is vertical preferably. After completing 8 reps have a partner lift the weight for you and resist the lowering of the weight to a count of 8. Repeat.

Back

- machine pullover- 1 set of 12 reps + 6 static holds

Adjust the machine for your height so full movement can be done. On most machines, place your elbows on the pads alongside the pullover arm. Your hands should rest lightly on the front of the bar being careful not to grip the bar tightly. As you lower the arm behind your head breathe deeply and get a good stretch in your lats before exhaling and bringing the arms down in front of you until it is just above your thighs.

After hitting failure at 12 reps, increase the weight slightly and bring the arm down in front of until you are at the spot where maximum contraction occurs and hold the arm in that position for 10 seconds. Rest 10 seconds then repeat for a second 10 second hold. Finish the set by completing four more holds.

- machine rows mid-position- 1 set of 12 partial reps

Select a weight that is moderate and use the middle handles on the machine. Divide the movement into three equal zones. Do three reps in the first zone, three in the middle zone and finish by doing three reps in the final zone. The

advantage of using a rowing machine instead of a barbell is that it supports your back against a pad instead of relying on the back to support itself. The machine forces you to use good form instead of jerking the weight as is common with barbell rows.

- cable pull-downs- 1 set of 12 reps + 6 static holds

Attach a pair of ab straps to a high pulley. Place your elbows in the straps as you sit facing the cable machine. Inhale as you get a good stretch in your lats as you lift your arms overhead. Exhale as you pull your elbows down to your sides and squeeze your lats hard. Continue until you have completed 12 reps. Increase the weight slightly and pull the ab straps three quarters of the way down and hold for 20 seconds. Return the weight to the stack and rest for 10 seconds. Repeat for a total of 6 static holds.

This exercise is converted from a compound movement to an isolation one by the use of the ab straps. By using them, most of the arm muscles are removed from the exercise, making the exercise focus on the lat muscles.

Shoulders

- seated machine laterals-1 set of 12 reps + several burn reps

I prefer machines, like the Cybex, where you face the weight stack as that facilitates rapid weight changes. Place your forearms against the shoulder pads and grip the handles lightly. The better you are at relaxing your grip and allowing your forearms to push against the machine's arms, the better you will be able to focus the resistance to your deltoids. Exhale as you push the machine arms up to shoulder level. Slowly lower the arms back down. After completing a total of 12 reps, do a series of short, rapid reps until you are unable to move the weight anymore.

- seated machine presses-1 set of 16 static holds pyramid style

Begin by selecting a weight that is moderately heavy. Press the machine arms to the point before lockout and hold for 20 seconds. Return the weight to the stack and rest for 10 seconds. Increase the weight by one plate and do a 20 second hold in the same position. Continue adding a plate and holding the machine arms in the same position until you have worked your way to a weight that you can barely hold for 20 seconds then begin working your way down the stack in the same way you worked your way up.

Biceps

- Nautilus overhead curl-1 set of rolling static partials with a time under tension of 65 seconds.

Use the Nautilus overhead curl machine, which does a great job of providing a very intense workout for your biceps due to the cam action and its angled position. Select a moderate weight and grab the handles after placing your elbows on the pads overhead. Curl the handles down halfway and do a series of burn reps. Let the handles up slightly and do a 10 second static hold. Let the handles up to the beginning and do a full rep. Continue doing a series of random burn reps and static holds in different positions of the rep interspersed with complete reps. Do the holds in random zones to work the biceps completely.

Rolling static partials are a creation of mine based on the benefits of burn reps, partial reps and static holds. Burn reps increase the intensity of a set by extending it past what normally would be possible by activating additional muscle fibers and causing more microscopic tears in the muscle.

Partial reps allow you to focus your training on different portions of a lift or train different zones of an exercise to allow you to use more weight when resuming full range of motion training. Static holds, as you can tell, are a favorite of mine due to their ability to increase the intensity of a set by forcing your muscles to contract hard against a heavy weight.

- machine curl-1 set of 12 negative-accentuated reps

Select a weight that leads to muscular failure at 12 reps. Curl the machine arms to the top and tense your biceps hard before lowering the weight down, focusing all of the weight on your left arm only. Repeat, this time placing all of the weight on your right arm as you slowly lower the weight. Continue alternating between your left and right arms until you have completed 12 reps.

Triceps

- seated machine triceps extensions-1 set of 12 negative-accentuated reps

Select a moderate weight, sit in the machine and place your elbows on the pad in front of you. Grab the handles and extend them in front of you until your arms are fully extended. Tense your triceps hard and lower the weight back down slowly bearing all weight onto your left arm. Repeat, this time placing all weight on your right arm. Continue until you have completed 12 reps.

- seated triceps dips-1 set of 8 static holds

Select a heavy weight that barely allows you to hold the arms of the machine in place for 20 seconds. Press the arms of the machine down to just prior to lockout and hold them in place for 20 seconds before returning to the top. It is important to sit upright to concentrate the work on your triceps. Repeat after resting for 10 seconds.

Abdominals

- ab crunches-1 set of 15-20 reps

Adjust the seat position so the padded arm connects with your chest area. Cross your arms in front of you and lean forward as far as you can. You should have a strong contraction in your ab muscles. Let the weight back to the stack and repeat.

- side crunches-1 set of 15 reps

Sit sideways in an ab crunch machine. Press the arm forward with your side as far as you can before returning to the beginning. After finishing 15 reps with your left side switch and train your right side the same way.

- leg raise machine-1 set of 15 reps

Use a standing leg raise machine which has no weight stack so there is nothing to adjust with the exception of the height of the bench. Grab the handles, lean back and raise your legs up as far as you can. Complete a total of 15 reps.

- wrist curls on bicep curl machine-1 set of 15 reps

Sit in the machine and do 15 reps with a palms-up grip.

- reverse wrist curls-1 set of 15 reps

Same as above, except use a palms-down grip.

All of the routines above make use of high intensity principles and require an intensive effort. Don't finish the set until you have hit muscular failure or else you will fail to receive the full benefit of this training. Because the machines are designed to train your muscles more effectively than other tools, a low set count is all that is needed to maximize both strength and size development.

Exercise variety with machines

One of the concerns with using machines exclusively is the lack of exercise variety. For instance, triceps training, if station machines are used, offer seated triceps extension, dips and overhead triceps extensions. I may have missed a machine, but that is all that is typically offered. The best method to remedy this is to add in cable machine exercises as they add in a near limitless variety of exercises.

Another advantage of cable machine exercises is they don't limit your exercises to a fixed plane of movement like single station machines do. Cable exercises imitate many dumbbell exercises and offer freedom of movement like dumbbell exercises do.

For chest training you can add in lower, middle, upper cable crossovers, cable bench presses and cable upward chest crossovers. Cable exercises for the back include cable rows, straight-arm cable pull downs, pull-downs, ab strap pull-downs and angled cable pull-downs.

Cable exercises for the arms are almost unlimited and include cable curls, concentration cable curls, seated rope curls mid-pulley, rope curls high pulley, rope curls low pulley, cable preacher curls, palms-facing pull-downs, overhead triceps extensions, low pulley triceps extensions, angled triceps extensions, press-downs, push-downs and more. You get the idea-cable machines and cable exercises are a great addition to any machine training program.

Cable machine routines

Legs

- cable squats-1 set of 15 reps

Attach a cable from the low pulley to a weight/dip belt. Stand slightly wider than shoulder width and keep your back straight while looking up at the wall in front of you. Inhale deeply while squatting down as far as you can. Exhale as you press yourself upward avoiding a lockout at the top. Repeat for a total of 15 reps.

- cable lunges-1 set of 12 reps per leg

Attach the cable from the low pulley to a weight/dip belt. Stand shoulder width apart and take a deep step with your left leg. Bring the leg back and repeat with your right leg. That counts as one rep. Complete 11 more.

- low pulley hip inward sweep-1 set of 15 reps

Attach a cable from the low pulley to an ankle attachment on your left leg. Standing sideways to the machine, bring your left leg inward with a sweeping motion until across the center of your body. Repeat for 15 reps before switching to your right leg and completing 15 reps.

- low pulley hip outward sweep-1 set of 15 reps

Attach a cable from the low pulley to an ankle attachment on your left leg. Standing sideways to the machine, bring your left leg outward with a sweeping motion until at the far left of your body. Repeat for 15 reps before switching to your right leg and completing 15 reps.

- cable calf raises-2 sets of 20 reps

Attach a cable from the low pulley to a weight/dip belt. Step onto a wood block and lower your heels down to get a full stretch. Flex them hard as you bring your heels up as far as you can. Repeat.

Chest

- cable crossovers high pulley-1 set of 12 reps + burn reps

Attach a handle to the high pulley on both sides of a cable crossover machine if possible, or to do this exercise one arm at a time, on the high pulley on a single cable machine. Stand in front of the machine and inhale deeply while bringing your arms back as far as you can to get a good stretch. Exhale as you bring the handles diagonally down in front of you, ending at thigh level. Tense your pec muscles hard before returning. Repeat for a total

of 12 reps before performing a series of short, rapid reps until unable to move the handles any further.

- middle pulley upward crossovers-1 set of 12 reps + burn reps

Attach a handle to the mid pulley on a cable machine. Stand with the machine on your right side and bring the handle upward across your body until it is even with your left side at shoulder level. Tense your pec muscle hard before slowly lowering the handle. After reaching failure at 12 reps do a series of burn reps until unable to move the handle. Switch hands and train your left side.

- incline machine cable bench presses-1 set of 8 reps + 5 forced reps

Select a weight that leads to failure at 8 reps. After completing those have your training partner apply enough assistance allowing you to do 5 additional reps.

Back

- cable machine rows rest-pause- 1 set of 8 reps

Select a weight that is near or at your 1RM. Row the handles to your chest as you exhale. Inhale as you return the weight to the stack. Rest 10 seconds as you reduce the weight slightly and complete a second rep. Continue until 8 reps have been completed.

Rest-pause was designed to be an efficient way to use maximum weights while preventing failure due to the buildup of lactic acid in the muscles. The rest period is brief but is long enough to allow the removal of lactic acid and the infusion of new blood and nutrients, making it a very effective variable for both strength and muscle gains. Champion bodybuilder Mike Mentzer obtained great results while training for the Mr. Universe contest years ago.

- cable machine pull-downs-1 set of 8 reps + 4 forced reps

Use either a cable machine with a plate loaded bar or a selectorized weight stack. Most machines have a brace to place your legs under to hold you down during the exercise. Let the weight pull your arms up high to get a full stretch. Focusing the resistance on your lats, pull the handles down to your lower chest/upper ab area. Pause for one second then complete the next rep.

After finishing 8 reps have your partner assist you in the completion of 4 additional reps.

- cable machine stiff-legged deadlifts- 1 set of 15 reps + burn reps

After selecting an appropriate weight, stand shoulder-width apart while keeping your knees locked. Bend over until the handles almost touch the floor. Lift the handles up deadlift style until standing erect. After completing 15 reps do a series of burn reps until unable to move the weight anymore.

Shoulders

- cable front deltoid raises-1 set of 15 reps

Sit or stand in front of a cable machine after attaching a handle to the low pulley. Keeping your arm slightly bent, raise the handle up directly in front of you until it reaches shoulder height. Lower the handle back down slowly.

- bent-over deltoid raises-1 set of 15 reps

Bend over until parallel with the floor while holding a handle attached to the low pulley of a cable machine. Raise the handle out to your side until parallel with the floor. Repeat.

- cable machine presses-1 set of 8 reps + burn reps

These can be done one or two hands at a time. Sit in front of a cable machine with the handles attached to the low pulley. Press the handles straight up overhead, pause then return. After completing 8 reps perform a series of burn reps until unable to move the weight.

Biceps

- cable curls-1 set of 12 reps + burn reps

Do these one or two arms at a time for variety. Attach one or two handles to the low pulley of a cable machine and curl the handle(s) up to your chin. After 12 reps do a series of burn reps.

- cable pull-downs with palms-facing-1 set of 15 reps + 4 pure negative reps

After finishing 15 reps, have your partner lift the handles into position and lower the weight slowly to a count of 8. Repeat for a total of 4 negative reps.

Triceps

- standing cable push-downs-1 set of 15 reps + burn reps

Keep your elbows at your sides while pushing a rope or triceps handle straight down in front of you. Do a series of burn reps after finishing 15 reps.

- angled triceps extensions-1 set of 12 reps omni-contraction

Stand facing away from the cable with a rope handle attached to the high pulley. Lean forward and extend the rope handle at an angle overhead. Let the handle descend one third of the way and do a static hold for 10 seconds before lowering to mid point and holding for 10 seconds. To complete the rep, lower the handle to the bottom and hold for 10 seconds. Repeat.

Abdominals

- standing ab crunches-1 set of 15 reps + burn reps

Stand with your back facing the machine while holding a rope handle attached to the high pulley. Using your ab muscles only, lean forward and crunch your abs toward the ground. Repeat. Do a series of burn reps until unable to move.

- cable side bends-1 set of 20 reps per side

Stand to the side of the machine while holding a handle attached to the lower pulley. Lean away from the machine as far as is comfortable and complete 20 reps before switching sides.

- cable situps-1 set of 20 reps + burn reps

Sit on the floor in front of a cable machine while facing away from it after attaching a rope handle to the low pulley. Hold the rope handle behind your head and do a sit up. It will be necessary to have a partner hold your legs down as you do this exercise.

These exercises are all practical for toning, strengthening and building muscle. As you can see cable machines add a vast array of useful training exercises to your machine training. As a rule I don't use cable machines

exclusively during a training session. Instead I use a combination of free weights, station machines, multi-station and cable machines. Approximately 90-95% of my workouts are comprised of machine exercises as I find them to be the safest, most practical and one of the most effective tools for building strength and muscle.

Circuit Training with Weight Machines

While it is possible to do a circuit training routine with free weights, it is much easier to construct a circuit training routine using selectorized weight machines, whether its with station or cable machines. The fast changing of resistance and ease of moving from one machine to the other lends itself to this type of training.

Training with circuits builds aerobic endurance as well as strength due to the fast pace of the training. Initially one circuit is done, and as the trainee becomes more experienced, an additional circuit or two is added. We need to use a rational amount of exercise volume and avoid adding too much exercise or it will become necessary to "hold back" our efforts to complete the high volume training. If you desire to occasionally add additional exercises or volume that will be OK as long as it is temporary.

During each exercise go to muscular failure, ending a set when you are unable to complete another rep. There should be no rest between exercises to keep your heart rate up and work your muscles hard in a short period of time. Once you progress to more than one circuit rest 1-2 minutes after each circuit before beginning the next one.

Beginner's Circuit Routine

- leg press-1 set of 15 reps
- bench press-1 set of 10 reps

- machine rows-1 set of 8 reps
- machine presses-1 set of 10 reps
- ab crunches-1 set of 15 reps

After using this routine for two weeks progress to this intermediate routine.

Intermediate Circuit Routine:

- leg extensions-1 set of 15 reps
- lat pull-downs-1 set of 12 reps
- machine dips-1 set of 10 reps
- machine presses-1 set of 10 reps
- machine shrugs-1 set of 10 reps
- machine rows-1 set of 8 reps
- machine bench presses-1 set of 10 reps
- ab crunches-1 set of 15 reps
- leg raises with machine-1 set of 15 reps

Perform one circuit of this program while in the intermediate program. To progress to the advanced level you should have been training with the intermediate program for 4 weeks.
The following is a great advanced routine:

Advanced Circuit Routine:

- leg extensions-1 set of 15 reps
- leg presses-1 set of 10 reps
- pek dek-1 set of 12 reps
- machine Bench press-1 set of 8 reps
- Nautilus pullovers-1 set of 12 reps
- machine rows-1 set of 8 reps
- machine presses-1 set of 10 reps
- machine shrugs-1 set of 10 reps
- machine curls-1 set of 10 reps
- seated machine triceps extensions-1 set of 10 reps
- ab crunches-1 set of 15 reps
- leg raises with machine-1 set of 15 reps

Initially complete one circuit. After training with this routine for a while, you may do a partial second circuit after a 2-3 minute rest. Never do a total of more than18 sets. This training will give you a complete muscle building workout and will get you in great condition at the same time with no additional aerobic training needed.

There are additional machines available that we haven't used during the programs thus far but that are valuable additions to any workout. Included in these are donkey calf raise, Nautilus behind neck, rotator, abductor, adductor, hip and back, squat and chin/dip assist to name a few.

New machines are being brought to the market by reputable companies all the time so keep in tune with the industry to see which ones you might like to include in your machine training programs. There are also machines that are not so good being brought to market by second-rate companies that haven't bothered to invest the proper research monies into their development and design which can make them both dangerous and counter-productive.

Some more suggestions

I feel the best way for most weight trainees to train is to use a combination of free weights and weight machines because they both offer advantages. Free weights, especially dumbbells, offer the most natural movement and force your body to balance the weights. This is great for building full range strength.

Weight machines, whether selectorized or plate-loaded, are designed to force you to exercise with your muscle's ideal strength curve which allows you to isolate all of the resistance to the muscle being trained. This is largely due to the machine eliminating the need to balance the weight and the action of the cam or pulley system. The point is both free weights and machines have their advantages. While I make good use of free weights, I prefer the advantages of machines.

Since the weight machine's cam keeps the resistance even throughout the movement, in most cases the sticking point is eliminated. There is no point during a machine exercise where the resistance leaves the muscle unlike some free weight exercises.

Using the barbell or dumbbell curl as an example, when you begin curling, the weight feels heavy and peaks at midpoint. As you curl further the resistance is removed from the muscle because of mechanical leverage.

All of the resistance is removed from the biceps at the top of the movement, which takes away all muscle building stimulus. As you can see, the standard free weight curl leaves a lot to be desired. The machine curl corrects this problem by changing the leverage and providing a constant resistance level via an engineered cam.

Because of this I recommend eliminating the standard curl in favor of the machine curl. This is true in other exercises as well. My rule of thumb is if I

have a machine that I can use instead of free weights, I'll use the machine in most cases. I do like to use free weights for variety though.

List of machines

Nautilus Pullover

This is the granddaddy of weight machines and was the first Nautilus machine to hit the market and remains the most popular one today. It is very effective at removing the arm action from the pullover and isolating it to the lats, where its supposed to be. The seat is adjustable and can accommodate most adults.

It uses Kevlar belts which don't stretch,run smoothly and last a long time. The weight stack is more than adequate for all but the strongest of individuals. To use this machine, sit in the seat and belt yourself in. Step on the foot pedal to bring the arm to the front of you. After placing your elbows on the pads let the foot pedal loose which places all weight on the arm. After getting a full stretch exhale and bring the arm down in front of you.

Nautilus Mid-Row

This machine allows the user the freedom to define his/her own path of motion during the exercise, while the handles rotate freely, allowing the user to set natural wrist rotation. The weight stack offers plenty of weight which

is driven by Kevlar belts. Using a machine like this is great for people that have back injuries due to the support the machine affords the back.

Nautilus Lat Pulldown

This machine has rotating handles which allow the user to move the handles in a way that minimizes strain on the wrists,preventing injury. It is great for isolating action to the lats. The cam on this machine reminds me of the first generation Nautilus machines.

Nautilus Incline Bench Press

This machine adds safety and smooth operation to the incline bench press. It uses Kevlar belts like other Nautilus machines. The angle of movement is perfect and you have a couple of choices for hand placement which changes the movement slightly. I like the traditional positioning but prefer the grip that is parallel to your body. The weight stack provides plenty of resistance.

Nautilus Vertical Bench Press

This machine uses Kevlar belts throughout for smooth operation. I like the seated position for this exercise as opposed to the lying version that Nautilus initially produced. Like the incline version there are two hand positions available. The weight stack provides sufficient amount of weight for even the most advanced user.

Nautilus Dip Machine

I really like the ability this machine gives you to do zone partials as well as loading up the weight for heavy reps and static holds. Lean forward to train chest and remain upright to work your triceps. This machine features a 310 lb weight stack driven by Kevlar belts so it offers durable and quiet operation.

Nautilus Bicep Curl Machine

This machine uses Kevlar belts to provide smooth operation and durability. There is more than ample weight on the stack to provide even the most advanced user with a heavy workout. This machine places the user's arms at a higher angle than most machines, which provides an intense contraction at the end of the movement. This model is great for zone partials,rolling static partials and static holds.

Nautilus Standard Bicep Curl

This is the standard curl machine from Nautilus. Kevlar belts are used to add smooth operation and durability. The stack has plenty of weight for the advanced user, and like other Nautilus machines, is easy to change weight fast. The engineered drive pulley system offers the user an ideal strength curve to develop the biceps.

Nautilus Nitro Pec Squeeze

This machine is great for isolating your pec muscles and has a large weight stack that is more than adequate for even the most advanced trainee. Place both arms over the pads and bring them down in front of you. Squeeze your pecs hard before returning. This machine is great for all types of training from full rep,negatives,zone partials,rolling static partials and static holds.

Nautilus Ab Crunch Machine

This machine is great for isolating and training the entire ab region with a concentration on the upper portion. As you do this exercise relax your face and all muscles other than your abs so the full effect is on training your abs. Select a moderate weight and do a rep count between 15-25 to strengthen and tone your abs. Keep the set count between 2-3 to strengthen the muscle and forget about burning fat off with high reps/sets because it is impossible to spot reduce.

Nautilus Reverse Ab Crunch

This machine isn't common and you may not see one in your gym but may be able to purchase a new or used one for your home gym. Put your feet under the pads as shown and curl the handles up with your abs in an ab crunch motion. Use moderate weights and reps.

Nautilus Rotary

This machine is a great compliment to the ab crunch, reverse crunch and leg raise machines. It focuses efforts on the oblique muscles located at the side of your midsection. Use a moderate weight/rep protocol to strengthen and tone this area without adding too much additional muscle. Grab the handles while sitting in the machine, lean against the pads and twist side to side.

Technogym Lower Back

This Technogym brand lower back machine isolates weight resistance to the lower back muscles safely, allowing intense training without injury. The seat is fully adjustable to allow users of all heights to use the machine. When training with this machine use a controlled motion throughout without any momentum to avoid injury.

Nautilus Leg Extension

This machine effectively isolates the quad muscles allowing the user to do full reps, zone partials and static holds. There is more than ample weight on the stack.

Nautilus Leg Curl

There are three different varieties of leg curl machines, standing,seated and lying. The one pictured here is the seated model. All three are equally effective at producing excellent results.

Nautilus Leg Press

This is a well-engineered machine with a large weight stack to accommodate the most advanced user. The angle of motion and the leverage of action help the user to build maximum muscle and power quickly.

Donkey Calf Raise

The donkey calf raise machine eliminates the need to have training partners sit on your back while you are performing the exercise. The weight stack is expansive due to one's ability to use heavy weight while training with this exercise. Using this machine gives you a very balanced exercise as compared to the manual version.

Hip Abduction

This machine combines two machines into one, hip abduction and hip adduction, made possible because of the adjustable pads. These exercises are great for building up hip strength which is important for daily life as well as performance in other lifts.

Other high quality machine manufacturers

There are many manufacturers of selectorized and plate-loaded machines, some of which were mentioned previously. They are Cybex, Strive, Icarian, Hoist, Matrix, Bodypower, Freemotion, Technogym, Med-ex and over 100 more. You can be assured of getting a good machine if you purchase one of these brands.

Look for machine sturdiness, durability and proper smooth operation. Make sure the machine has a proper cam or leverage pulley system to give the proper strength curve for the muscle its designed for. Take your time to test the machine's operation and avoid rushing into a purchase.

All-In-One or Multi-Station Machines

A very good addition to any commercial or home gym is the multi-station machine because it allows many different exercises to be done on a single machine. A typical setup is a bench press station, a leg extension/leg curl, pec fly, pull-down, low, middle and high pulley. Many also contain a press station and leg press. You can save substantial money over purchasing a series of single station machine circuit and the machine's footprint will be a lot smaller.

These machines range from single weight stack home models to 4-6 weight stack commercial models with 6-12 different stations. One thing to consider is the number of people using the machine at the same time. For each additional person using the machine at the same time you will need to purchase a model with an additional weight stack.

Because of the close proximity of the different machine stations, it is easy to rapidly move from one exercise to the next, which is ideal for high intensity or circuit training.

This is a basic multi-station gym and features a plate-loaded weight bar, pek dek, bench press, high pulley, low pulley and leg extension/curl. It is designed for one user.

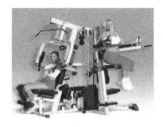

This mid-level multi-station gym has the same features as the basic model plus a leg raise and dip bar platform.

This advanced multi-station gym has many additional stations added from what the mid level multi-station gym has. There is an incline sit-up bench, leg raise bars, leg press attachment and more. This enables you to set a gym up literally with one large machine station instead of a series of individual station machines. It is impossible to correctly cam the machines to reflect the strength curves for each individual muscle but machines like this are great to train with because of their smooth operation and versatility.

Pre-exhaust routines

One of my favorite high intensity variables is pre-exhaust training. With this method you can train a muscle past the point of muscular exhaustion. One of the most important factors in training to develop new muscle growth and strength is to end a set at failure, when you are unable to complete an additional full rep in good form.

With pre-exhaust we can go one step further, ending our training of a muscle beyond muscular failure. The key is the structure of the exercises. Typically, a muscle is trained with two exercises. The first one is an isolation exercise, the second is a compound one. Each exercise is done with one set each to failure.

The secret is to wear out the muscle with the first exercise, which trains the target muscle only. The second exercise uses fresh assistance muscles that help the target muscle be pushed past normal failure. Do both exercises with no rest in-between them or you will lose much of the effectiveness of this variable. This is because when a muscle rests as little as 3 seconds it regains 50% of its strength.

Using the chest muscles as an example, we will do the following workout:

Chest

- pek dek- 1 set of 12 reps + burn reps

Select a weight that causes you to hit failure at 12 reps. After completing these do a series of burn reps until unable to move the machine arms at all.

Pek dek-start   finish

- incline bench press- 1 set of 12 zone partials + 3 forced reps

Select a weight that enables completion of 12 partial reps done in this manner: Do three reps in the bottom third zone to failure, reduce the weight and do three in the middle zone to failure, reduce the weight and do three in the top zone to failure. After finishing these have a partner assist you in completing three forced reps. The advantage to using partial reps is you train each portion, or zone, of an exercise to failure multiple times instead of once like you do during normal style sets.

Back

- Nautilus pullovers- 1 set of 12 reps + 4 static holds

After going to failure with 12 reps, increase the weight and do 4, 10 second static holds with a 10 second rest in- between.

- pull-downs palms-facing- 1 set of 10 reps omni-contraction + burn reps

Do 10 omni-contraction reps to failure before completing a series of burn reps until unable to move the weight.

As an alternative to this workout you may do the following routine:

- stiff-arm pull-downs- 1 set of 12 reps + 6 static holds

Attach a straight bar attachment to a high pulley on a cable machine. Stand in front of the machine and bring the bar down to your lower thighs while keeping your arms locked straight. After hitting failure with 12 reps, do six, 10 second static holds with a 10 second rest in between. Use varied positions in the range of movement for the holds. Adjust the weight as necessary to make the holds a maximum effort.

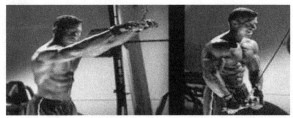

stiff-arm pull-downs-start   finish

- seated machine rows- 1 set of 8 reps + 4 forced reps

Go to failure at 8 reps and complete 4 forced reps with the assistance of a training partner.

machine row-start   finish

Shoulders

- seated lateral raises- 1 set of 12 reps omni-contraction
- seated machine presses- 1 set of 12 static contraction holds

Select a weight that is about 80% of your max and do a 10 second static hold. After resting 10 seconds, increase the weight to 90% of your max and do a second 10 second hold. Continue working up the weight stack until you reach the maximum weight you can hold for 10 seconds. Reduce the weight and work your way back down the stack.

Or this routine:

- cable front deltoid raises- 1 set of 12 reps + burn reps

Do a series of burn reps at the end of the set.

cable front raise-finish

- seated machine presses- 1 set of 8 reps rest-pause

Do 8 rest-pause single reps with maximum weight. Rest 10 seconds between reps. Change the weight as necessary to facilitate the completion of the set.

Biceps

- machine curls- 1 set of 12 zone partials

Complete a set of a total of 12 partial reps, 3 in each zone. Go to failure in each zone, reduce the weight and train the next zone.

- Seated cable rows palms-up- 1 set of 8 reps + 4 static holds at the end of the set

Attach a short straight bar to the low pulley on a cable machine. Do 8 reps in the typical fashion. Increase the weight and do a total of 4, 10 second static holds, reducing the weight as necessary.

Triceps

- Seated triceps overhead extensions with rope handle- 1 set of 10 reps + 4 pure negative reps

Attach a rope handle to the mid pulley. Face away from the machine and extend the rope overhead. Make sure to keep your elbows at the side of your head throughout. After completing 10 reps to failure, have a training partner lift the weight for you while you lower it to a count of 8 for each of 4 negative reps.

cable triceps ext-start   finish

- Close-grip machine bench presses- 1 set of 6 reps extra slow speed

Use a rep cadence of 10/4, 10 seconds to lift the weight followed by a 4 second negative. When you train with a slow speed you will feel like you are exercising in slow motion. Once you become experienced with this method, you will come to appreciate the variation this gives your training.

Legs

- Leg extensions-1 set of 15 reps extra slow

Use a rep speed of 10/4, ten second positive and four second lowering phase. At 15 reps you should have reached muscular failure.

Leg extension-start   finish

- Leg press-1 set of 12 reps negative-accentuated

Using a moderate weight, complete 12 reps negative-accentuated style. Remember to place the entire weight on your left leg for the initial negative, then your right leg for the second. Alternate this for the entire set.

Leg press-start   finish

This exercise is demonstrated on a plate-loaded angled leg press machine. The traditional leg press machine used in years past had the user lying underneath the weight. I had one in the past, and while I benefited from it, the one drawback is the increase in thoracic pressure due to the heavy weight being overhead. This was prevented by folding one's arms across the chest, thereby relieving the pressure. I like the machine pictured here but prefer the selectorized machine because of its ease of use and safety.

The Super-X Hold Variable

We have been using static holds throughout this book as an effective method to increase the intensity of our machine bodybuilding training. Because of the heavy weights used and the high amount of muscle fibers recruited during the hold, it is a very effective way to build strength and add to muscle size.

To vary the training holds and continue producing better results, I regularly use different time periods for the holds. The most common hold time, which we have been using, is 10 seconds. With Super-X training, we will use 15,20,30 and 40 second hold times. Rest periods between holds is always 10 seconds because that allows the lactic acid to be flushed away by the blood and nutrients to be replenished into the muscle.

The use of extended hold times to further increase the intensity

I have formulated workouts using hold times longer than advocated by other static contraction practitioners. The 10-40 second hold times we will be using during the initial phase of this program will be staggered in an effort to initiate a favorable response from our central nervous and muscular systems and experience new muscle growth.

As you increase hold times you tire out muscle fibers you have been using to hold the weight and activate new fibers. In addition to muscle fiber stimulation, longer hold times cause an in increase in the sarcoplasmic fluid, which is the fluid surrounding the muscle fibers that is responsible for a major part of the hypertrophy of a muscle. Each hold time necessitates a different level of resistance which affects muscles in different ways.

In addition to different hold times, we have several different structures of training available such as the pyramid hold system, isolation contraction, compound contraction and the rolling static partials hybrid.

Workout 1-Chest
- Incline bench press- 1 set of 8 holds

1st hold-10 seconds 2nd hold- 15 seconds 3rd hold- 25 seconds
4th hold- 30 seconds 5th hold- 40 seconds 6th hold- 30 seconds
7th hold- 20 seconds 8th hold- 10 seconds

Workout 2-Chest
- Decline bench press- 1 set of 8 holds

1st hold- 10 seconds 2nd hold- 15 seconds 3rd hold- 25 seconds
4th hold- 30 seconds 5th hold- 40 seconds 6th hold- 30 seconds
7th hold- 20 seconds 8th hold- 10 seconds

Each muscle is trained with one exercise which is performed for one set of 8 holds of varied time frames.

Training Muscles with a Super-X Static Holds Variation

Up to this point we have using static holds at the end point of a movement but are going to change things up a bit. The end point, which is the place where the maximum amount of muscle fibers are engaged, is a great location to do a static hold. Another point in an exercise that's great to maximize a static hold's effectiveness is the point where you typically have a sticking point in an exercise.

In the curl, for instance, the bar usually stops at mid-point when a heavy weight is used. In the bench press, the bar tends to stop at mid-point as well, when the triceps become heavily involved in the lift. This is the area we are going to be focusing on. When we train with this very limited range of motion the plates on the weight stack rise only 2-4 inches.

This allows us to safely use very heavy weight to train with which will quickly exhaust the muscle(s). It necessitates limiting the range of motion of an exercise to the sticking point of an exercise instead of the endpoint like we have been doing.

Using the leg press as an example, after loading the weight stack with a weight much heavier than normal, push the footplate forward until the weight plates come up off the stack two inches and hold the weight for 20 seconds before returning the weights back to the stack. Quickly reduce the weight by 10 lbs. and repeat.

It may be necessary to attach a 10 lb. barbell plate to the stack via a plate attachment or add an accessory plate to the top of the stack. This is because most leg press machines have 20 lb. plates on their stacks. Continue working down the stack in 10 lb. increments until you have completed 10 holds.

This is what the workout looks like using a starting point of 600 lbs.

- 1st hold with 600 lbs for 20 seconds
- 2nd hold with 590 lbs for 20 seconds
- 3rd hold with 580 lbs for 20 seconds
- 4th hold with 570 lbs for 20 seconds
- 5th hold with 560 lbs for 20 seconds
- 6th hold with 550 lbs for 20 seconds
- 7th hold with 540 lbs for 20 seconds
- 8th hold with 530 lbs for 20 seconds
- 9th hold with 520 lbs for 20 seconds
- 10th hold with 510 lbs 20 seconds

This session consisting of 10 holds is a complete workout for the upper leg, so no more exercises are needed. The two important points to consider are to put forth maximum effort and to place your feet up high on the footplate to include the hamstring muscles in the movement otherwise it will be necessary to train them separately with leg curls or stiff-legged deadlifts because it is imperative to have balanced development between the frontal and rear leg muscles to prevent injury.

To complete our leg workout we need to train our calf muscles in the following way:

Assuming a starting weight of 800 lbs, the workout is as follows:

Standing calf raises-1 set of 10 Super-X Static Holds

- 1st hold with 800 lbs for 20 seconds
- 2nd hold with 790 lbs for 20 seconds
- 3rd hold with 780 lbs for 20 seconds
- 4th hold with 770 lbs for 20 seconds
- 5th hold with 760 lbs for 20 seconds
- 6th hold with 750 lbs for 20 seconds
- 7th hold with 740 lbs for 20 seconds
- 8th hold with 730 lbs for 20 seconds
- 9th hold with 720 lbs for 20 seconds
- 10th hold with 710 lbs for 20 seconds

As with all Super-X Static Hold workouts, maximum effort is needed to thoroughly train the muscle(s) with no rest at all taken between holds with this variation. The brief time it takes to change weight is ample to flush the lactic acid from the muscle and send new nutrients in to replenish it.

calf raises on machine

Super-X Static Hold Arm Workout

Bicep cable curl- 1 set of 8 Super-X Static Holds

- 1st hold with 100 lbs for 20 seconds
- 2nd hold with 90 lbs for 20 seconds
- 3rd hold with 80 lbs for 20 seconds
- 4th hold with 70 lbs for 20 seconds
- 5th hold with 60 lbs for 20 seconds
- 6th hold with 50 lbs for 20 seconds
- 7th hold with 40 lbs for 20 seconds
- 8th hold with 30 lbs for 20 seconds

Cable curl- lift the weight off the stack 2-3 inches

Depending on how strong your biceps are you might need to keep the weight higher than the weights suggested. Another factor that comes into play with the arms is the amount of other training that they have been involved in. For instance, chest training utilizes the triceps and back training uses the biceps. If these muscles have been trained recently you may need to scale back arm training until they have completely recuperated from this training.

This training is very useful for all muscle groups and will quickly generate new strength and size. Use the same template by substituting appropriate exercises for each muscle. Both isolation and compound exercises may be used. Try and stagger them, switching between both types of exercises.

Superslow Training on Machines

Ken Hutchins was an associate of Arthur Jones, the inventor of Nautilus Machines. He reasoned that since it was advantageous to train with a slower form of training, that it would be better to train even slower.

Rep speed with traditional high intensity training is usually 2/4, two seconds to raise the weight and four seconds to lower it. Mr. Hutchins changed the rep speed to 10/10, ten seconds to raise and lower the weight. He later determined that the negative speed was too slow and allowed the muscle to rest briefly during the lowering phase. As a result, he increased the negative tempo to four seconds, thus changed rep cadence to 10/4.

One of the advantages of this slow method of training is the extremely low incidence of injury because heaving and jerking of weights is completely eliminated. The slow speed of the positive portion of the rep magnifies the resistance on the muscle, making it more intense. Four seconds on the negative phase is perfect for causing maximum overload of the muscle.

Some training practitioners might become bored because of the slow speed of the positive portion but once you have tried this training I think you'll agree that it adds new intensity to your training. Machines are ideal to use with this HIT protocol as they are with many of the other HIT variables.

To train with the correct time under tension we need to lower the rep count. For strength and muscle size development the ideal time under tension is 45-60 seconds. Since each Superslow rep takes 14 seconds to complete, to end a set at 45-60 seconds we will use 4-5 reps. Five reps takes slightly over 60 seconds,which is fine. Our set count will be two for small muscle groups such as arms and three for larger muscles like legs,back and chest.

Chest

- pek flye-1 set of 5 reps
- incline machine bench press-1 set of 4 reps
- seated dip machine-1 set of 4 reps

Back

- Straight-arm cable pull-downs-1 set of 5 reps
- Machine rows-1 set of 4 reps
- Reverse flyes-1 set of 5 reps

Legs

- Leg extensions-1 set of 5 reps
- Leg curls-1 set of 5 reps
- Leg press-1 set of 4 reps

Shoulders

- Seated lateral raises-1 set of 5 reps
- Seated machine presses-1 set of 4 reps
- Machine shoulder shrugs-1 set of 5 reps

Biceps

- Standing cable curls-1 set of 5 reps
- Seated machine rows with palms-up grip-1 set of 4 reps

Triceps

- Standing cable press-downs-1 set of 5 reps
- Seated triceps dips-1 set of 4 reps

Abdominals and lower back

- Seated machine crunches-1 set of 5 reps
- Standing machine leg raises-1 set of 5 reps
- Seated lower back extensions-1 set of 5 reps
- Standing stiff-legged cable deadlifts-1 set of 4 reps

Photo list of exercises

pec flyes- start

finish

Incline bench press on smith machine-start

finish

Stiff-arm pull-downs-start   finish

Cable rows-start   finish

Reverse Flyes-start   finish

Leg extensions-start

finish

Leg curls-start

finish

Leg press-start

finish

Cable lateral raise-start

finish

Standing cable curl-start

finish

Triceps push-downs-start

finish

Triceps dips-start

finish

Ab crunches-start

finish

Lower back extension-start

finish

Cable dead lift-start   finish

Types of Gyms

There are several types of gyms available to train in. Some gyms cater to free weight use only and are ideal for powerlifters and weight lifters. Other gyms have an even amount of free weights and machines and offer a good balance of equipment for most trainees.

Most gyms have a much higher percentage of machines compared to free weight equipment. Even though it is more expensive to purchase selectorized equipment than dumbbells and barbells, it is statistically safer to use machines, reducing the incidence of injuries and insurance claims.

There are newer gyms designed for strongman/strongwomen training. They contain specialized equipment like farmer's walk, tire flip, grip building and sleds for pulling power in addition to other pieces. This is one of the most rapidly growing "iron related" sports so these gyms are growing fast.

Final thoughts

Free weights,bands and weight machines all are useful tools to train with and each offer distinct advantages for training that the others lack. My experience has been the best method to use is to train with all of them to obtain the best results.

Free weights such as dumbbells, barbells and kettlebells allow the trainee to mimic the body's natural movements and are great for the development of raw power and balance. Barbells have limitations when it comes to leverage on certain movements like the barbell curl but are an excellent tool for building raw power and strength.

Dumbbells allow you to train your muscles using natural movements and build great functional strength. Kettlebells offer unique movements to train groups of muscles as well as the entire body as one unit and have been around for over 100 years. Weight machines became popular in the 1970's with the advent of Nautilus Machines and have the unique capability to isolate muscles and train them with the proper strength curve throughout an exercise with the use of a cam or engineered pulley system. Users are forced to train with the proper movement path, which prevents injury and maximizes strength and muscle size gains.

Certain machines, like the brand Strive, which is headquartered and made in Pennsylvania, have adjustable cams, which allow the user to change the strength curve of the exercise. This allows the peak contraction of an exercise to be focused on different zones to work past sticking points to build more strength overall in a muscle.

As far as acquiring commercial weight machines, the price of new machines many times is cost prohibitive but the used market offers them at a steep price discount compared to new pricing. There are many companies that specialize in the purchase, restoration and resale of these machines but the best place to get a good deal on these machines are places like eBay and Craigslist as well as gyms and schools that may be selling older models before they get the newest models.

Try and set your home gym up with one machine for each muscle group. Multi-station gyms replace many different machines and save a lot of money compared to the purchase of individual pieces.

If possible, try and purchase less common machines like a donkey calf machine and a seated shoulder shrug to add variety to your gym. If you don't have the budget to set up your own home gym, visit several commercial gyms in your area and join the one that offers the best combination of free weights and weight machines for a total body workout.

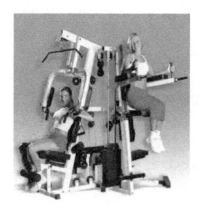

Bonus Material-Questions and Answers

You mentioned that you feel weight machines are superior to free weights for building muscle size and strength. Does that mean that you feel free weights are useless for building muscle size/strength?

I have found weight machines to be valuable tools for bodybuilding and fitness training because of their inherent safety, ease of changing weight, proper strength curve and smooth operation. Free weights are also wonderful tools to develop strength and power and have been proven effective for many years.

While they have some negatives like inefficient leverage in some exercises they make up for it by offering functional training exercises that mimic natural body movements. I recommend constructing training programs that have a healthy balance of free weights and machines.

In your book you have training routines with weight machines exclusive of dumbbells and barbells. Could you give some sample workouts using both weight machines and dumbbells/barbells?

Absolutely. Using free weights with machines is a great method to use the benefits of both tools to better your results. I use mostly dumbbells when it comes to free weights as they offer a better range of motion compared to barbells.

A great example of this is the bench press. If using a barbell, the range of motion at the bottom is limited by the barbell hitting your chest. Dumbbells allow you to lower the weights below chest level, giving a much better bottom stretch. Stretching has been shown to increase the strength output of a muscle because of increased muscle fiber usage.

Now lets take a look at a good routine for chest using weight machines and dumbbells.

- Pek dek flyes-1 set of 5 reps extra-slow reps
- Dumbbell incline bench press-1 set of 8 reps + 4 forced reps
- Seated dips-1 set of 8 reps + 3, 20-second holds

Here is a great arm routine:

- Machine curls-1 set of 10 reps + 3- 20-second holds
- Overhead rope curls-1 set of 10 reps omni-contraction
- Dumbbell rows-1 set of 10 reps

Is there enough exercise variety with weight machines? I don't want to become bored due to lack of sufficient exercises.

Don't worry, there are plenty of machine exercises for all muscle groups, including station and cable machines. For instance the chest can be trained using the decline bench press machine, vertical bench press machine,incline bench press machine, pek flye machine, Nautilus pec squeeze machine,low cable crossovers,middle cable crossovers and high cable crossovers and more. So you see there is no way to become bored with weight machine training.

What are the benefits of using/purchasing machines that are chain, cable and Kevlar driven?

All three drive linkages are very smooth and durable. Nautilus machines initially used chains to drive the weight stacks on their machines. They used cables briefly and have been using Kevlar belts ever since. Chains are very durable and provide years of use before any maintenance is needed. Cables provide smooth operation and are easy to repair or replace. Kevlar belts are commonly used because they are very durable and don't ever stretch.

I've heard that machines are great for building shape in a muscle but don't build much in the way of muscle size. Is this true?

These are very common misconceptions. Muscle shape is a result of genetics and is predetermined and can't be altered by training. Toning, building and defining a muscle will bring out the natural shape.

As far as weight machines' ability to build muscle, experience has shown that resistance used against a muscle properly will cause muscle size and strength gains. In fact, as we have discussed in this book, the resistance given by a weight machine is nearly perfect for developing muscle gains due to its cam and pulley system and the productive strength curve it offers.

Is there a good method to use weight machines if I am training for an upcoming power lifting meet?

Obviously it is extremely important to train with barbells if one is preparing for a power lifting competition. But is there a way to use weight machines to get a step ahead of the competition by developing more strength in the three power lifts?

The proper way to use machines for power lifting is to begin training with machines at the beginning of a contest prep schedule. This is the point where it isn't important to practice the three regulation lifts. The focus is the development of strength and power.

Use moderately heavy weights while training with machines at this phase. The exercises used should be a mix of isolation and compound movements. Compound exercises are ones that use more than one muscle group like bench presses, incline bench presses, presses and the like.

Isolation exercises are ones that focus the effort on muscles like biceps, triceps and shoulders while avoiding the involvement of helper muscles like triceps. A workout for bench press using this principle is:

- cable crossovers- 1 set of 12 reps

Use the high pulley attachment for this exercise. Bring the handles diagonally down in front of yourself, flexing hard at the end of each set.

- Bench presses partial reps- 1 set of 12 partial reps

Do a complete set of 12 full reps. Each rep should begin at the point of full stretch and power through to the pre-lockout position.

- Incline bench presses- 1 set of 10 reps.

Do full reps on this one.

- Standing bar dips- 1 set of 8 reps

This is a great basic workout to strengthen and build muscle. Now we will train with partial reps to train past sticking points. Using a vertical bench press machine load the weight heavy and press the arms in the middle third of the exercise until you are unable to move the machine arms. Reduce the weight and repeat, continuing this for several additional cycles. The rep count for each cycle should be in the 8-10 rep range.

Train various zones of the bench press in the same way. As you progress toward the contest, add more barbell bench pressing until it replaces the machine benching entirely. Use machines to perform triceps press downs and triceps extensions to strengthen those muscles in assisting the chest in bench pressing more weight. These exercises should be done after all bench pressing has been completed.

This strategy can be utilized for training the dead lift and squat in the same way using exercises like leg extensions, cable deadlifts, machine rows and such.

Thank you for purchasing this book. Be sure to check out my other books for more information on successful HIT bodybuilding and fitness training.

David Groscup

My contact information:

davidgroscup@gmail.com

http://drhitshighintensitybodybuilding.blogspot.com

CPSIA information can be obtained
at www.ICGtesting.com
Printed in the USA
BVHW020212280423
663222BV00009B/169

9 781496 039231